URBAN
CLOUDS

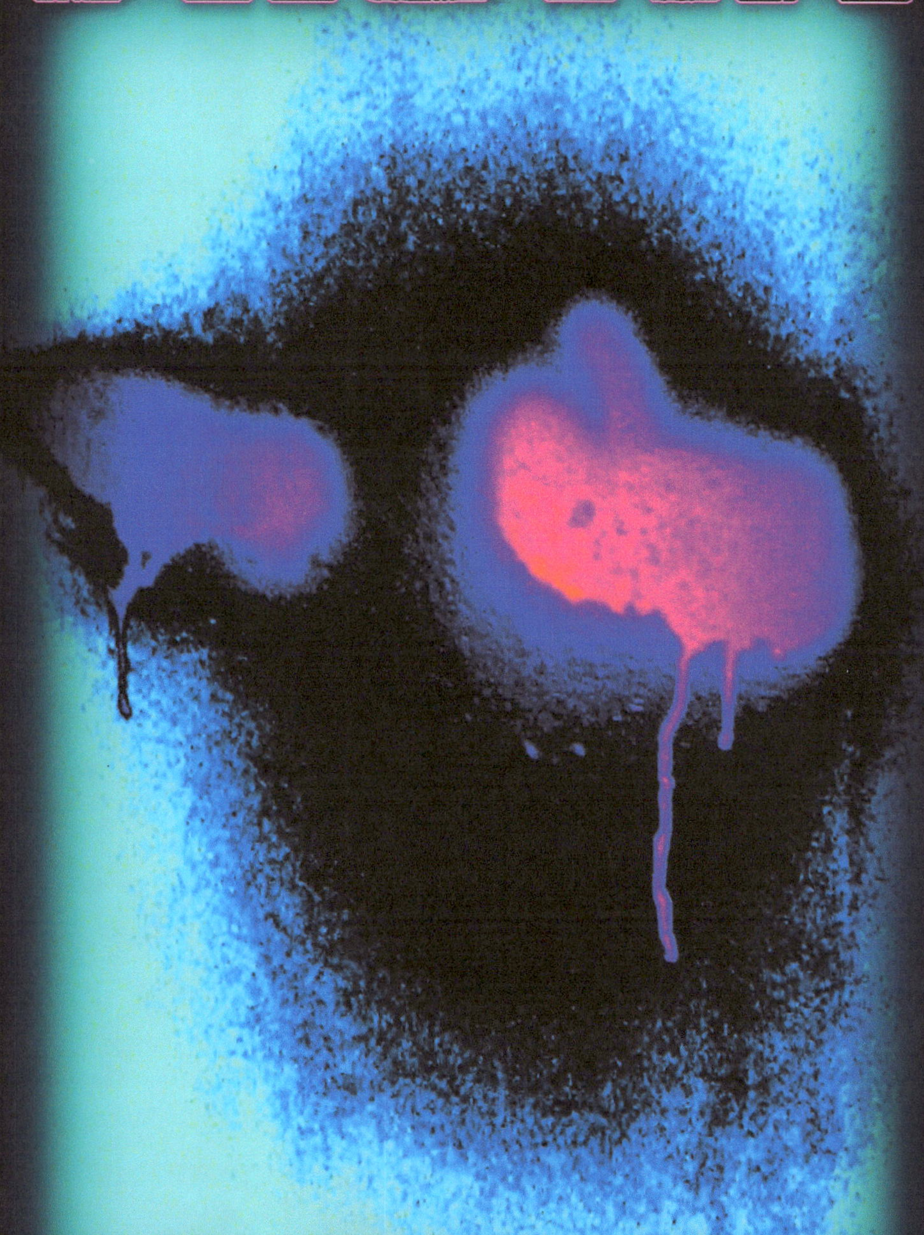

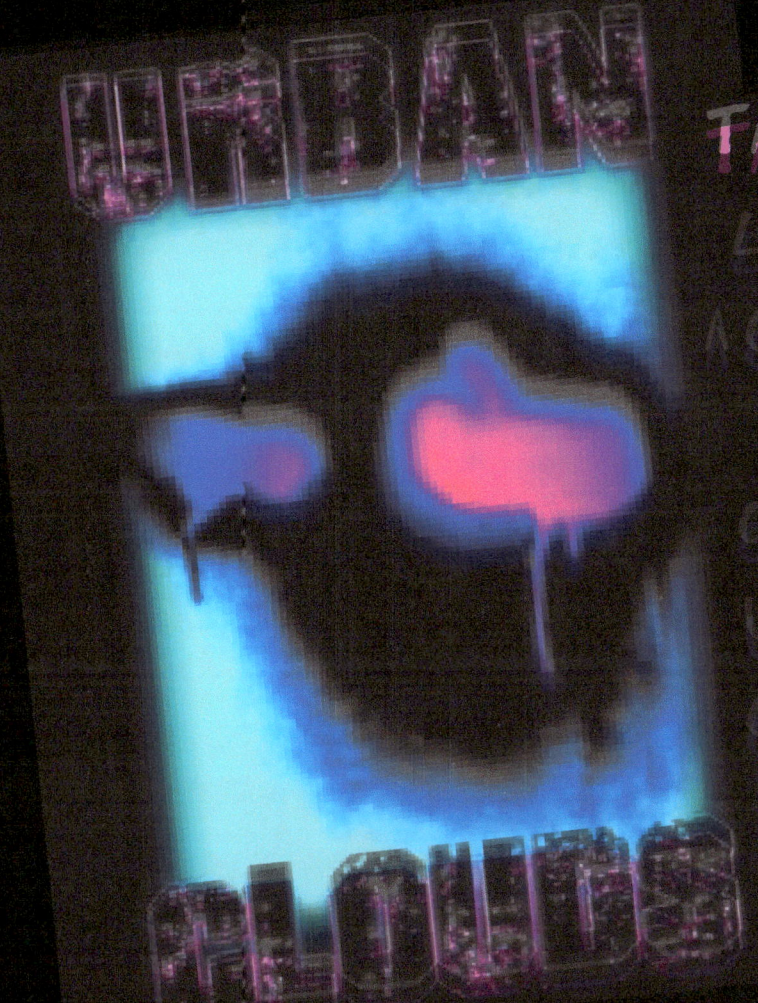

TABLE OF CONTENTS
LIFE IN A BIG CITY P3
A COMMON PROBLEM P4
URBAN CLOUDS P5
CLOUD SYMBOLISM P6
URBAN CLOUDS P8-22
CONCLUSION P23-24

ABOUT
BREEZE CANYON IS A SELF TAUGHT ARTIST FROM AOTEAROA, NZ. BREEZE MERGES PRIMITIVE AESTHETICS WITH MODERN ARTISTIC TOOLS TO CREATE ORIGINAL ARTWORKS IN TRADITIONAL MIXED MEDIA PAINTINGS, DRAWINGS, STENCILS, DIGITAL ART, VIDEO AND PHOTOGRAPHY.

ISBN: 9781795823968
ISBN: 9781795823968

Urban Clouds was written and produced by Breeze Canyon

Photography by Breeze Canyon

Poetry by Breeze Canyon

Original Table Banding artworks are all works included in the Urban Clouds project

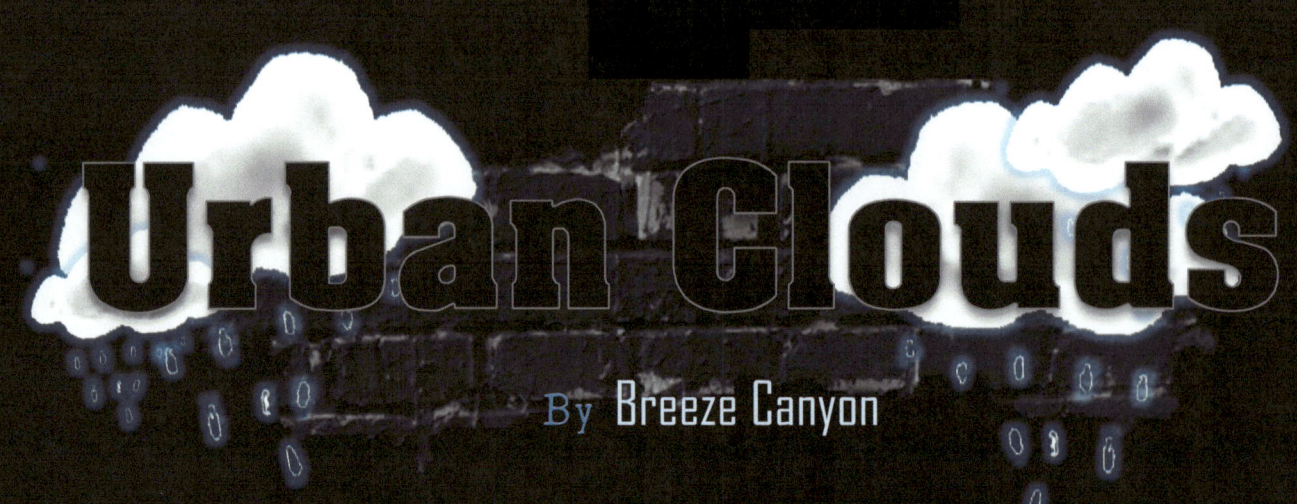

Urban Clouds
By Breeze Canyon

Life in a Big City

During the early morning hours of the day, while many are still fast asleep in their beds. The sound of street sweepers fill the frost chilled air. Their brooms swaying back and forth with a rhythmical precision of a time piece.

Well dressed office workers stream out of their domiciles into a maze of stairwells, footpaths and alleyways that stretch across the city.

Life, in all its abundant splendor, pulsates throughout the gigantic concrete jungle. However, it is easy to overlook one glaring visual eyesore that leaves more than just marks on the side of buildings.

The ebb and flow of life in a big city can best be explained with a series I call - <u>*URBAN CLOUDS*</u>

It's a unique perspective on an otherwise routine problem that plagues inner cities around the world. Urban Clouds is my take on the dualistic relationship between the municipalities and those seeking to get ahead.

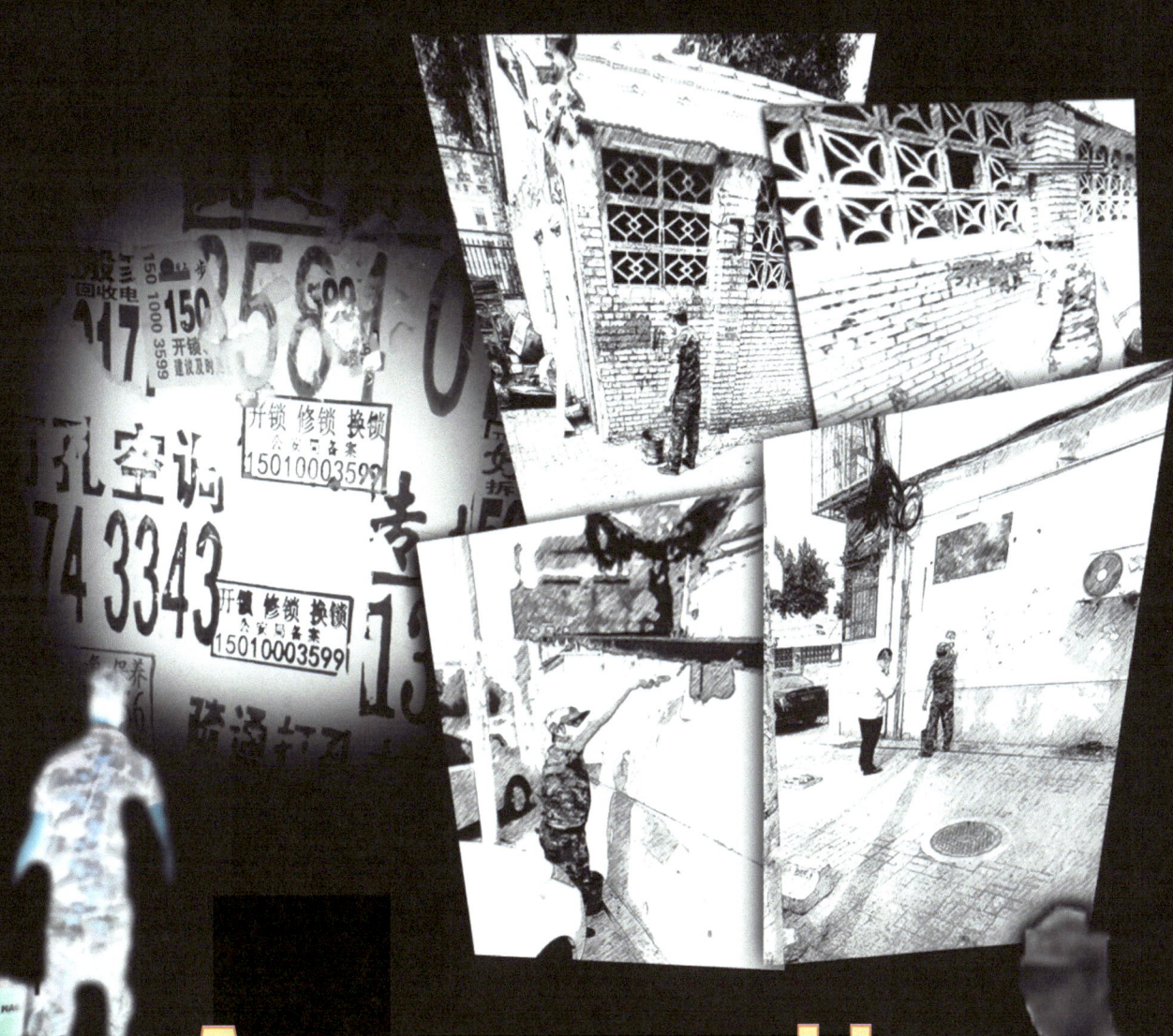

A common problem

GRAFFITI. IT CAN BE FOUND ALL OVER THE WORLD. ON SUBWAY CARRIAGES, TRASH CANS, BUS STOPS AND EVEN LIBRARY BOOKS. GRAFFITI IS OLD, TOO. ARCHAEOLOGISTS HAVE DATED SOME GRAFFITI AS FAR BACK AS PREHISTORIC TIMES. IMAGINE! GRAFFITI AS OLD AS THE SPHINX IN EGYPT!

IN TODAY'S WORLD, TACKLING THE ISSUE OF PUBLIC VANDALISM, WHETHER IT BE GRAFFITI, TAGGING, OR UNWANTED ADVERTISING, IS LEFT UP TO THE CITY COUNCILS, WHO OFTEN RELY ON A LARGE ARMY OF VOLUNTEERS AND HIRED GRAFFITI REMOVERS.

Expensive paint removers, anti graffiti paint and walls, security cameras and well placed street lighting have all been implemented at great length to combat what many deem as a scourge on society.

Urban Clouds

Urban Clouds is a way of seeing. It is my way of seeing something beautiful in the world around me. It is the way I view the coexistence between the different layers of society and its manifestation on the environment; or at least part of it. Let me explain.

I traveled throughout several major cities in Asia and discovered that unwanted advertisements were being covered over by city maintenance workers. These maintenance staff would use either a roller or more often a paint brush to completely cover numbers or stickers with paint.

The paint brush would be loaded with paint either gray, white or brown depending on the surface color; usually resulting in excessive dripping that oozed its way down the surfaces it covered.

In many instances, I noticed that it resembled a rain cloud. Everywhere I went I would look out for these rain clouds, or urban clouds, as I call them.

Cloud Symbolism

CLOUDS HAVE LONG HELD SYMBOLIC MEANING FOR CULTURES THROUGHOUT THE AGES. FOR EXAMPLE, IN ANCIENT ROME IT WAS BELIEVED THAT THE GODS THEMSELVES LIVED IN THE CLOUDS. ALSO ECHOING THIS SENTIMENT, MANY OF THE WORLD'S RELIGIONS ALSO TAUGHT THAT GUARDIAN ANGELS LIVED IN THE CLOUDS AND THAT CLOUDS WERE A GATEWAY TO THE HEAVENS.

IN EAST ASIAN TRADITIONS, SOME CULTURES VIEWED CLOUDS AS A SYMBOL FOR TRANSFORMATION, A CONCEALER OF TRUTH OR CHARACTER, A BRINGER OF GOOD THINGS TO COME OR OF BAD. CLOUDS ARE SEEN AS A SYMBOL OF PURITY AND OF HOPE. IT MAY ALSO BE INTERPRETED AS FOREBODING: AS A SADNESS, GRIEF OR OF IMPENDING DOOM.

<u>URBAN CLOUDS</u> ARE A SYMBOL OF MAN'S DETERMINATION AND WILL TO EXIST. THEIR PRESENCE IS A REMINDER OF THE CYCLICAL NATURE OF LIFE IN AN URBAN CITY. AS INDIVIDUALS PASTE, TAG AND SPRAY THEIR MESSAGES ON PUBLIC PROPERTY, THEY ARE COVERED OVER WITH PAINT.

THIS IS REPEATED OVER AND OVER AGAIN. THE CLOUDS APPEAR WHERE THERE WAS ONCE ADVERTISING. THE DRIPS OF PAINT LIKE A SHOWER ATTEMPTING TO WASH AWAY THE MARKS LEFT BY THOSE BEFORE. THE CONTINUAL BATTLE THAT WAGES BETWEEN THE CITY AUTHORITIES AND THE GROUPS AND INDIVIDUALS THAT STRIVE TO MAKE A LIVING CONTINUE TO THIS DAY AND WILL DO LONG INTO THE FUTURE. I HAVE CAPTURED SEVERAL HUNDRED OF WHAT I CALL <u>URBAN CLOUDS</u>. HERE ARE JUST A FEW.

I HOPE YOU'LL SEE IN THEM BEAUTY AND DETERMINATION, AND RECALL THE CONDITIONS THAT HAVE LEAD TO THEIR EXISTENCE. I'M GRATEFUL TO BE ABLE TO SHARE MY PERSPECTIVE WITH YOU. THANK YOU & GOOD LUCK. SINCERELY, BREEZE CANYON.

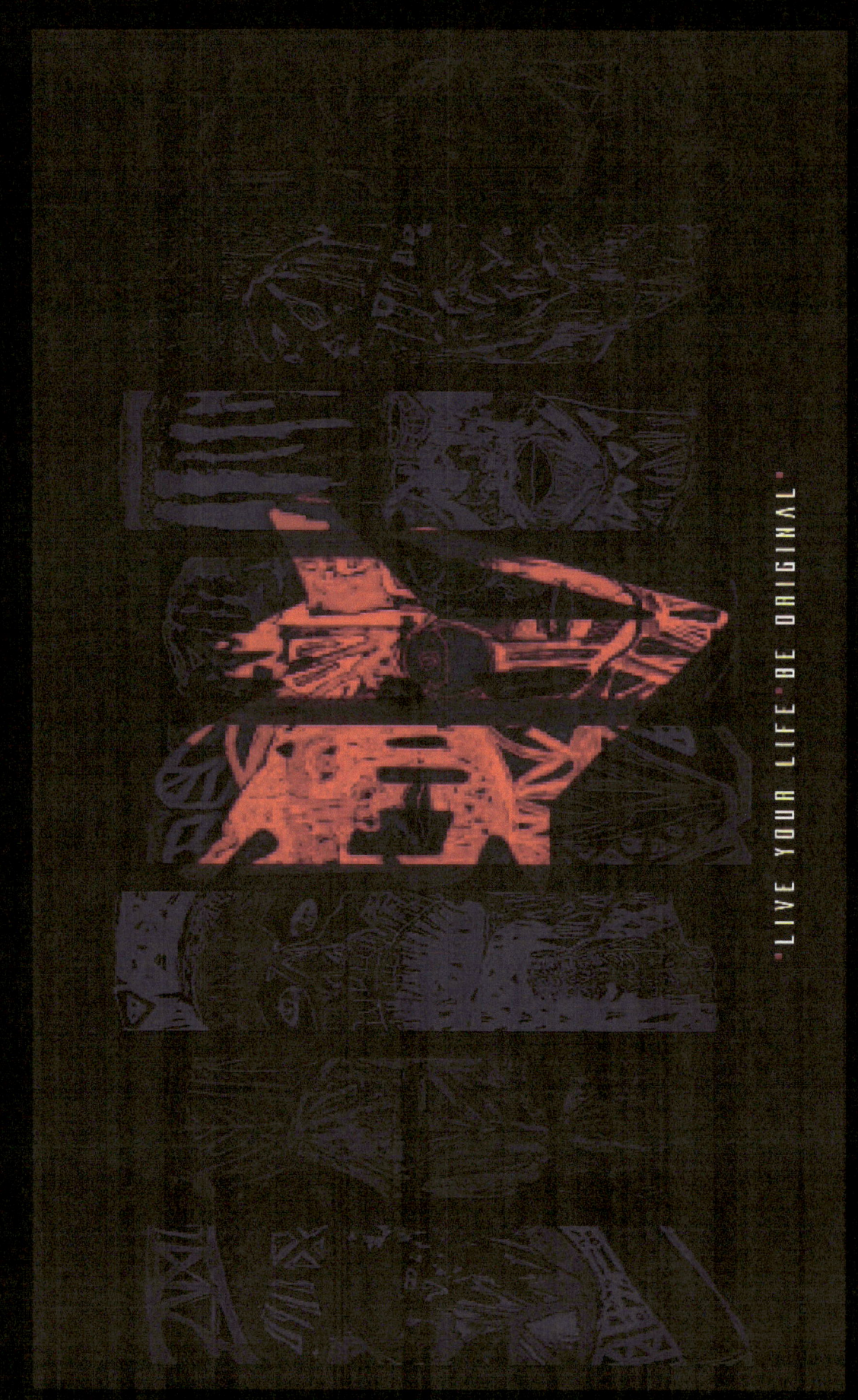
- LIVE YOUR LIFE - BE ORIGINAL -

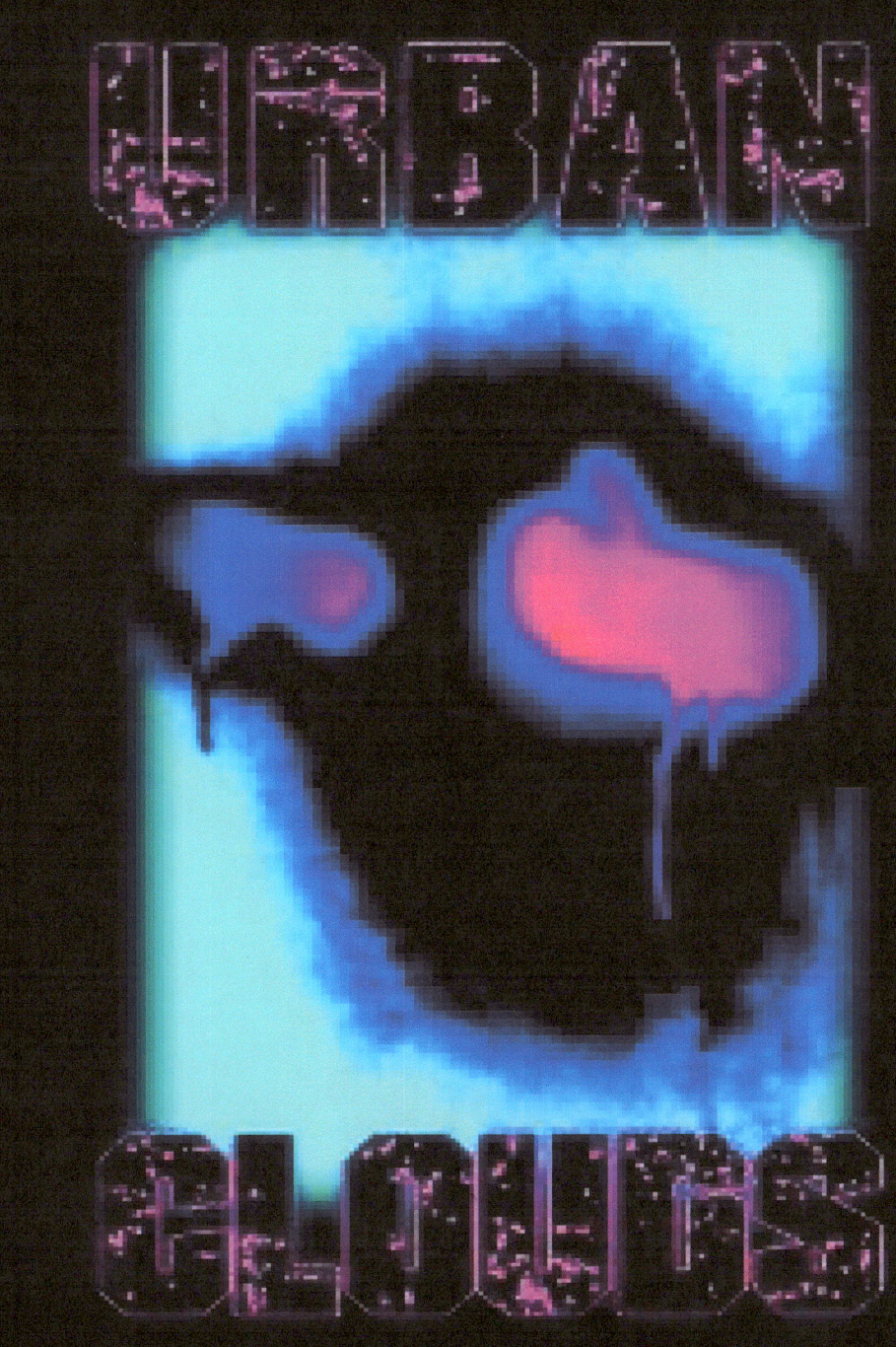

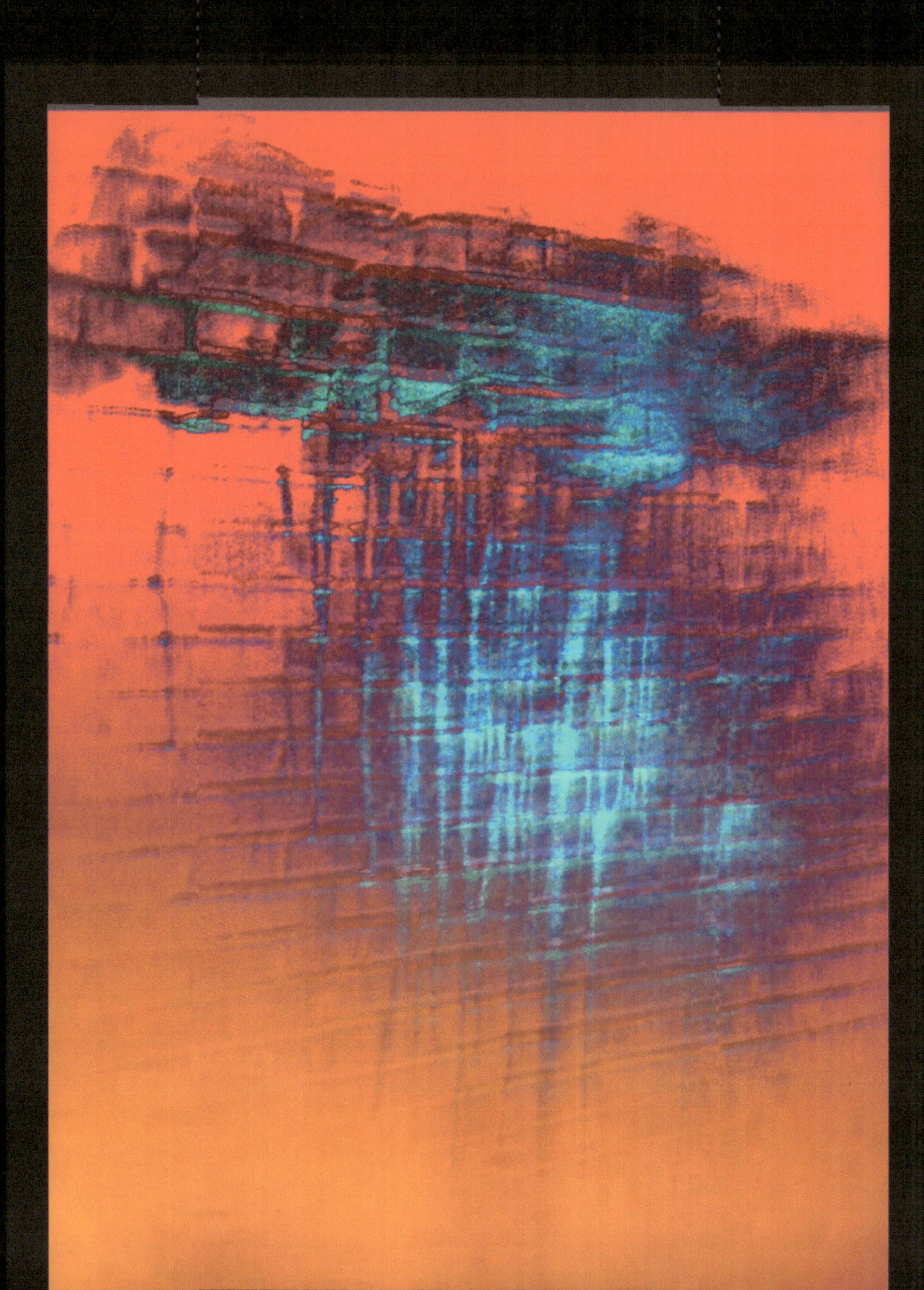

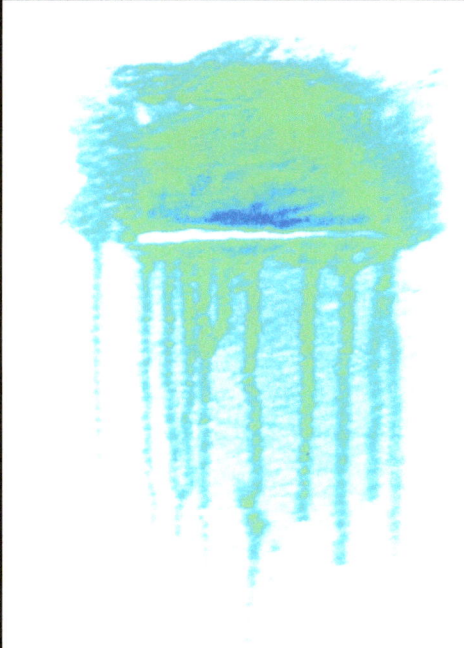

GRAY ARE THE DAYS, TOO FEW THAT REMAIN. LAYER UPON LAYER EACH ONE REVEALS WHAT HAS COME BEFORE, THOUGH SOME REMAIN CONCEALED.

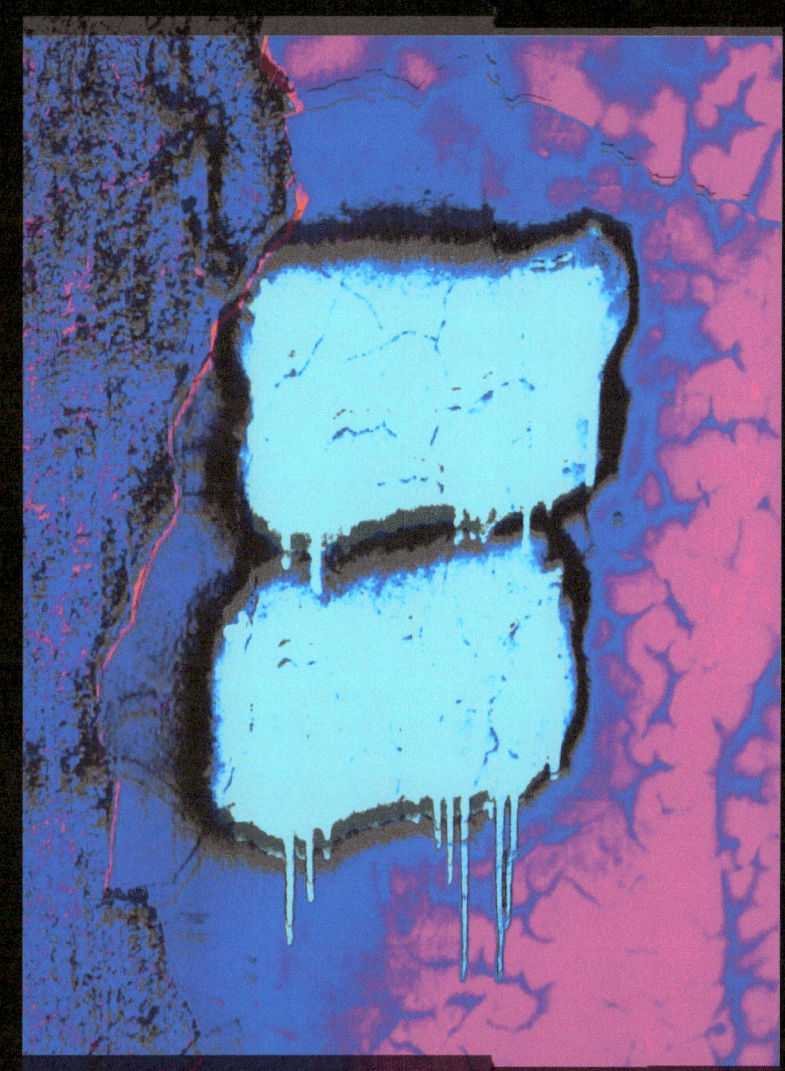

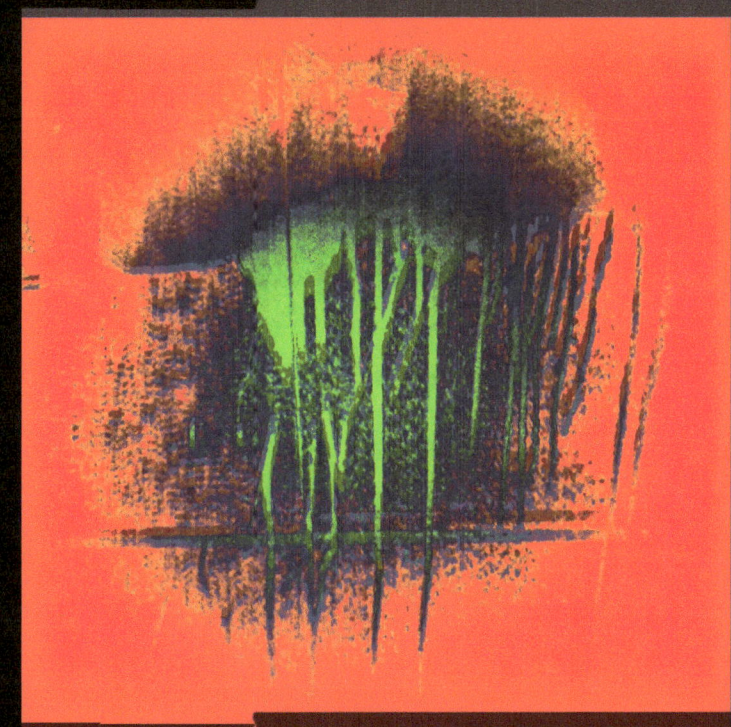

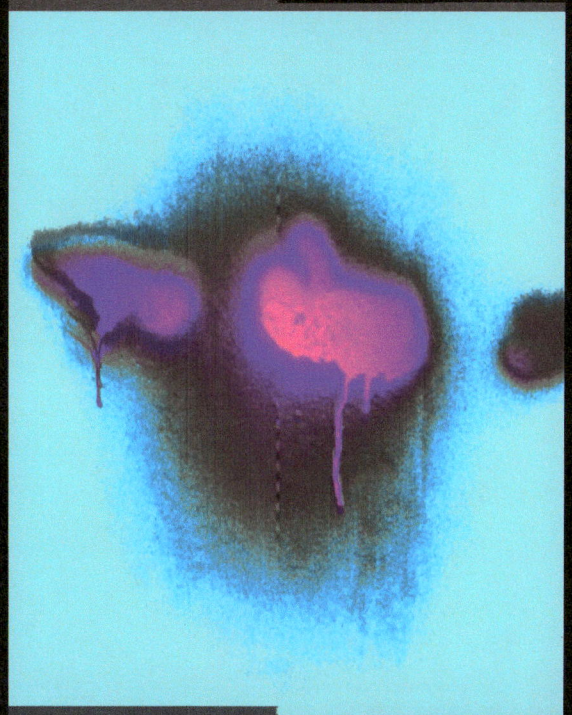

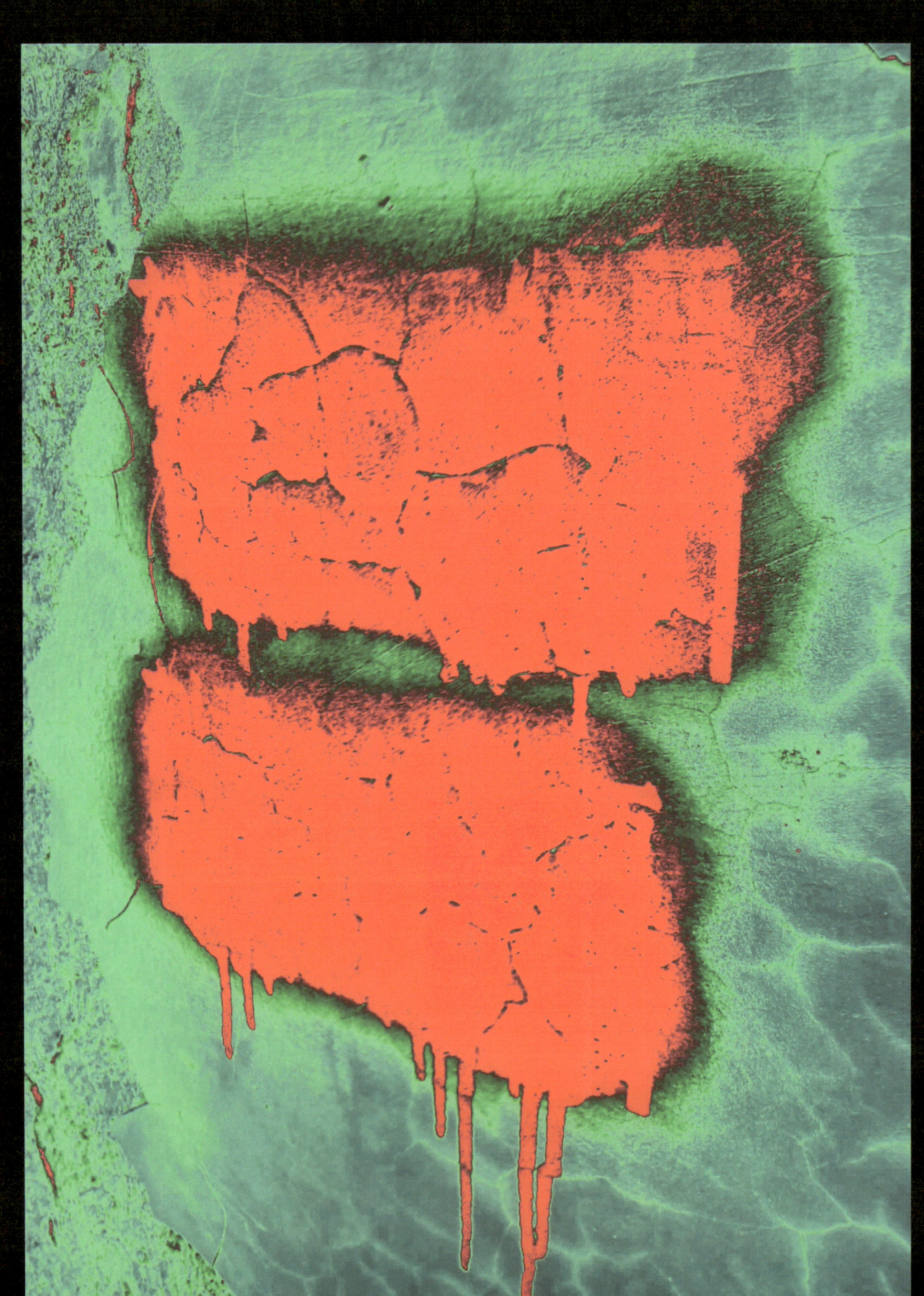

CLOUDS UPON CLOUDS AMASS THEMSELVES IN A VIRULENT DISPLAY ACROSS THE CITY. THEY SPAWN AND CHASE AWAY ALL THOSE THAT WOULD BE ENTICED TO PARLAY.

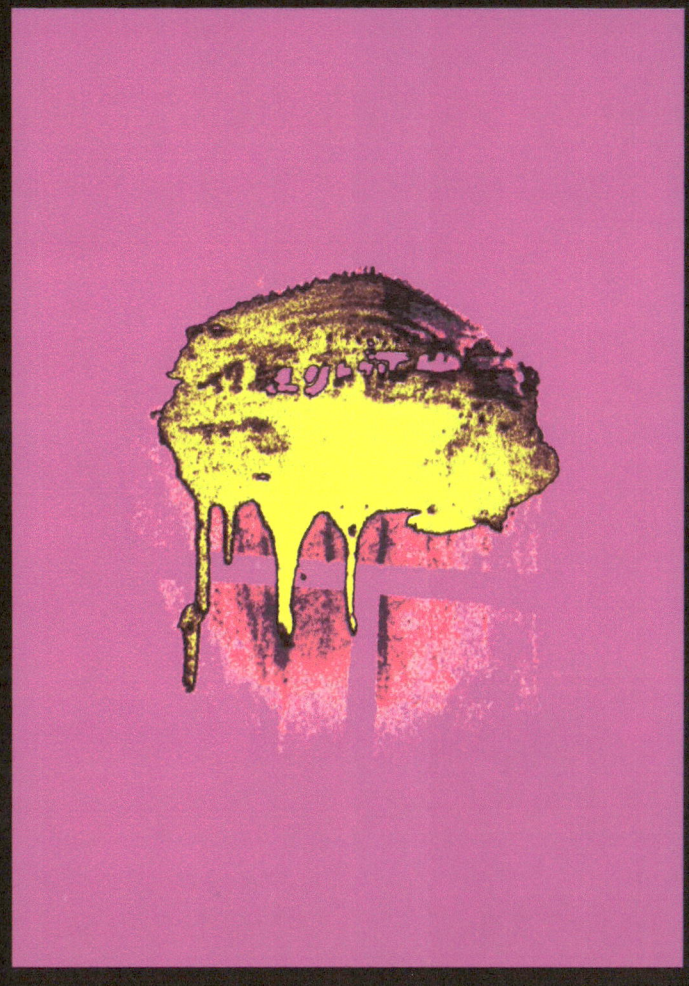
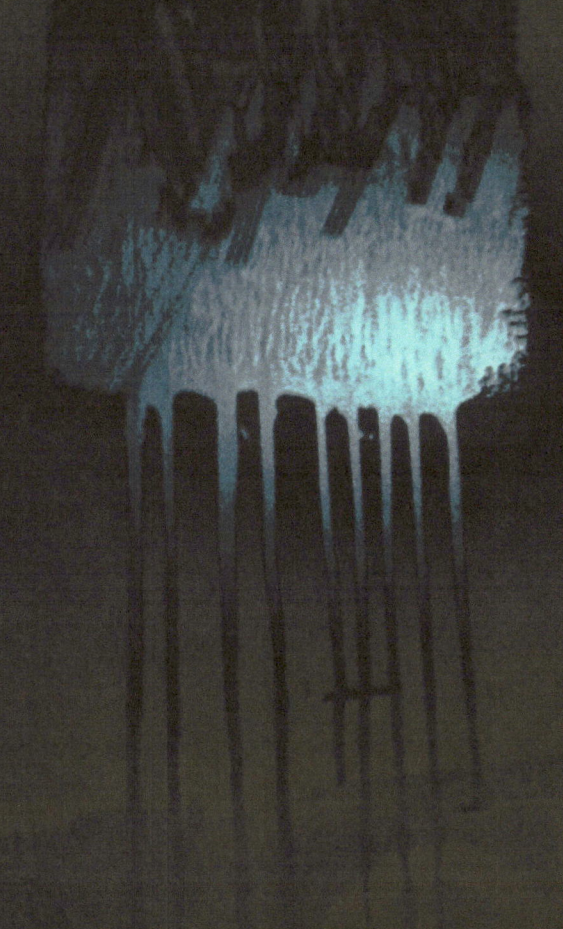
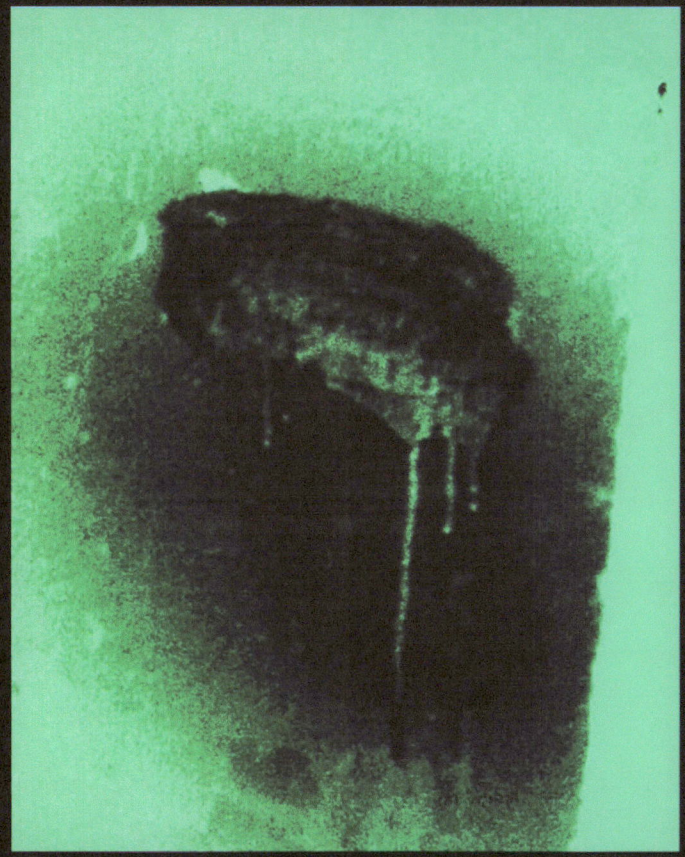

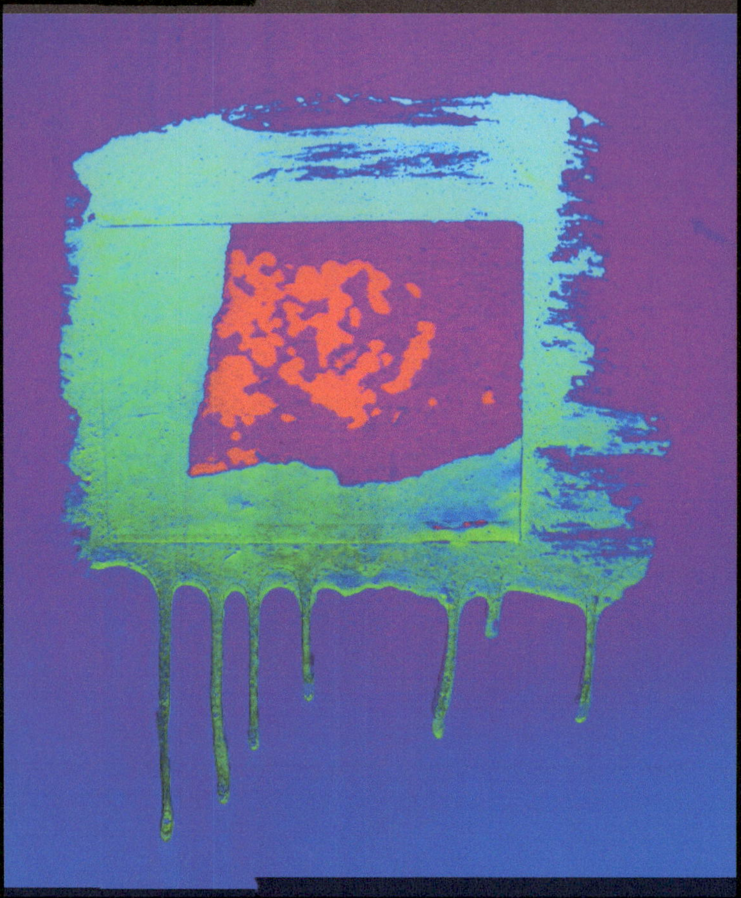

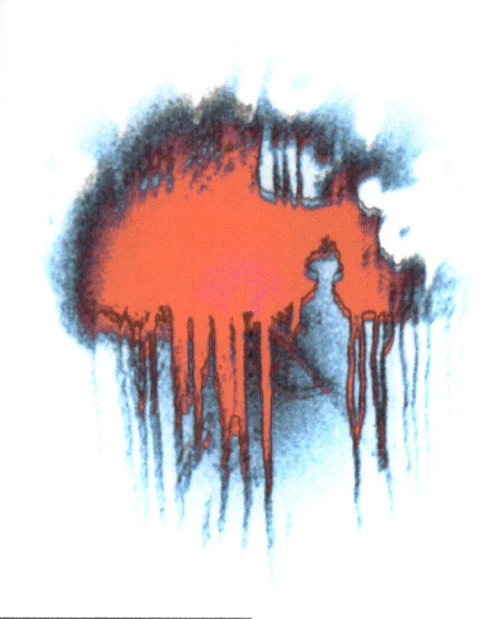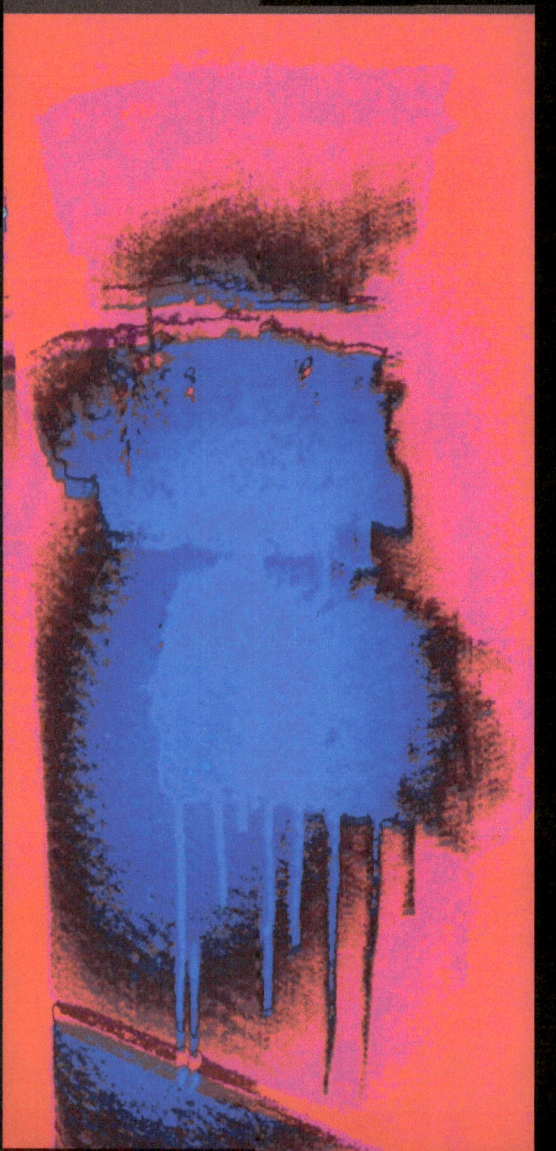

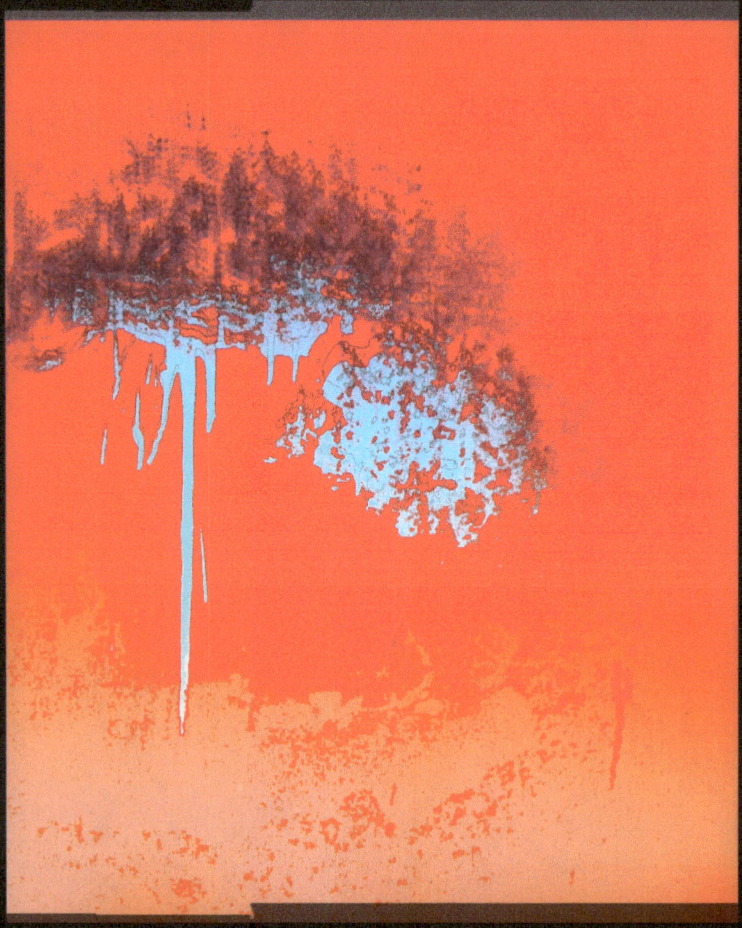

A DRIP, A DROP FROM ABOVE LIKE A VULTURE THAT LOOMS DOWN UPON A FADING LIFE BESET BY BURDENS OF TOIL OVER WHICH IT TRIES TO RELEASE ITSELF BUT CANNOT. ONLY MORE CLOUDS GATHER. DRIP, DRIP.

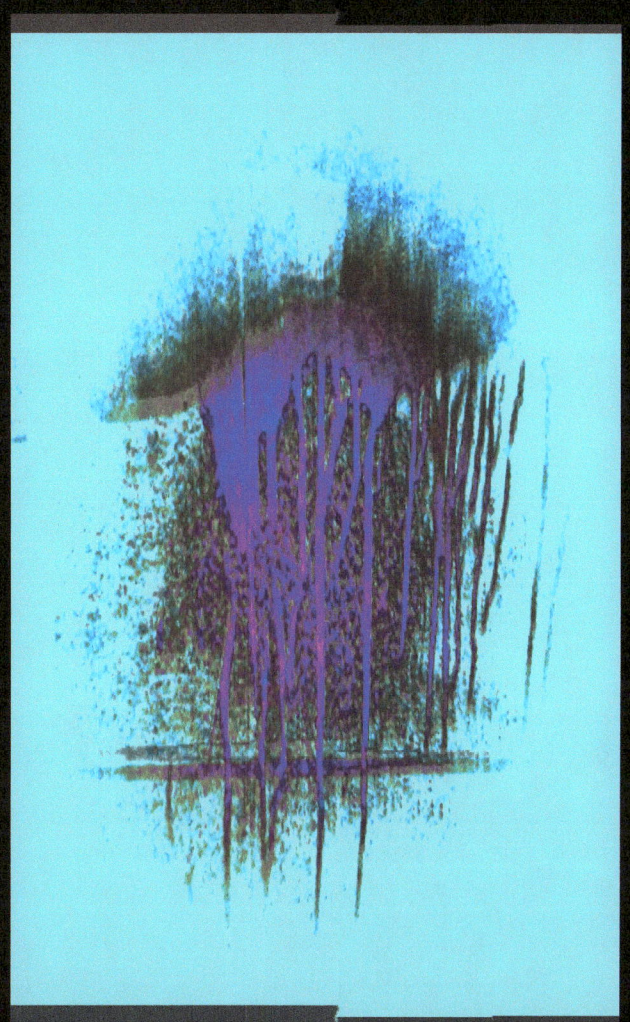
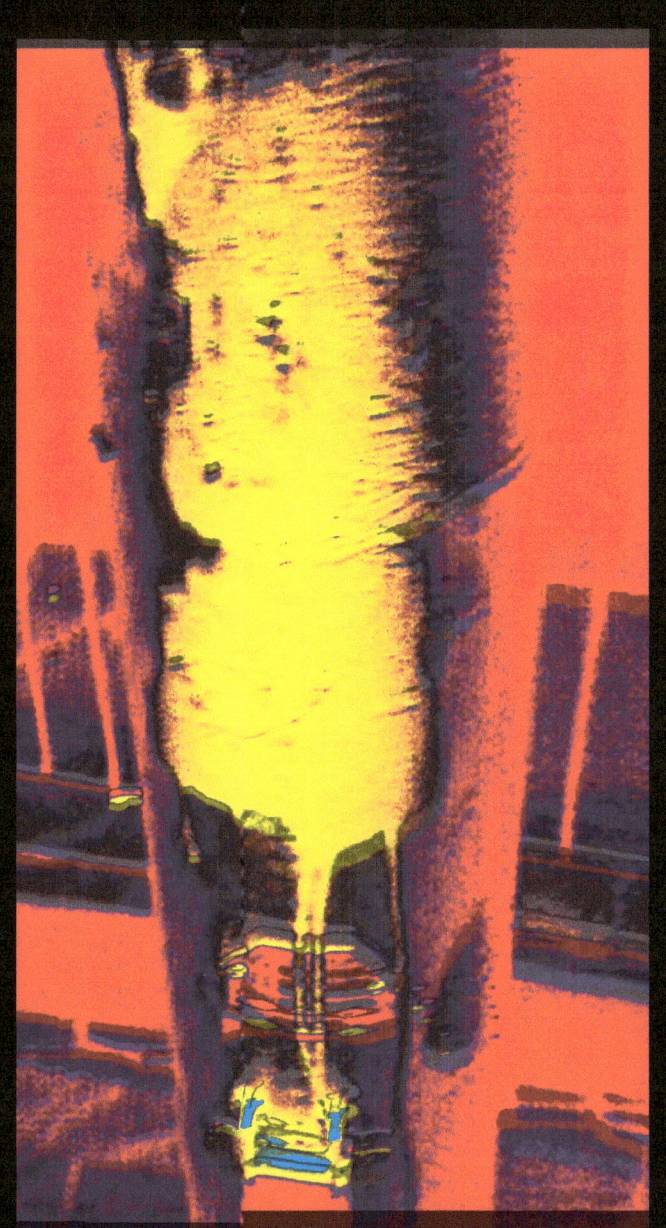
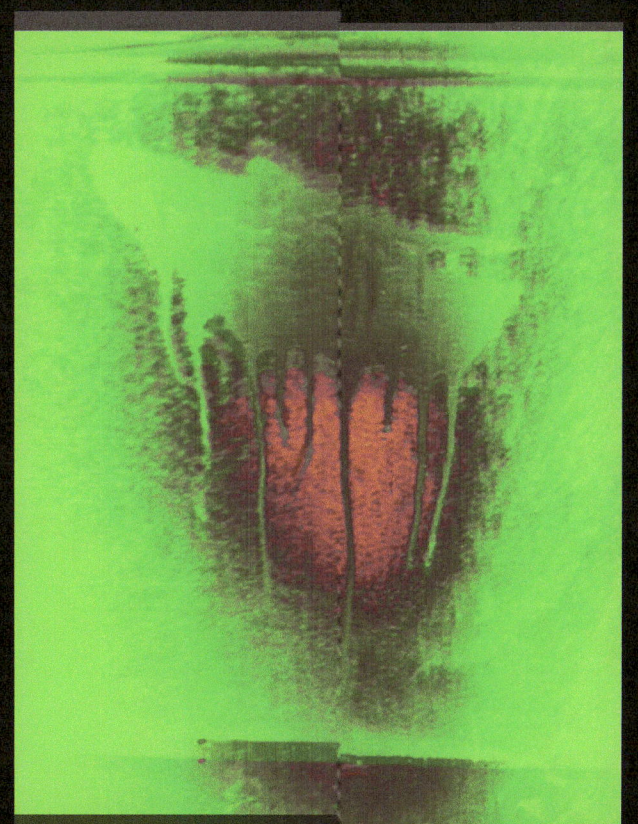

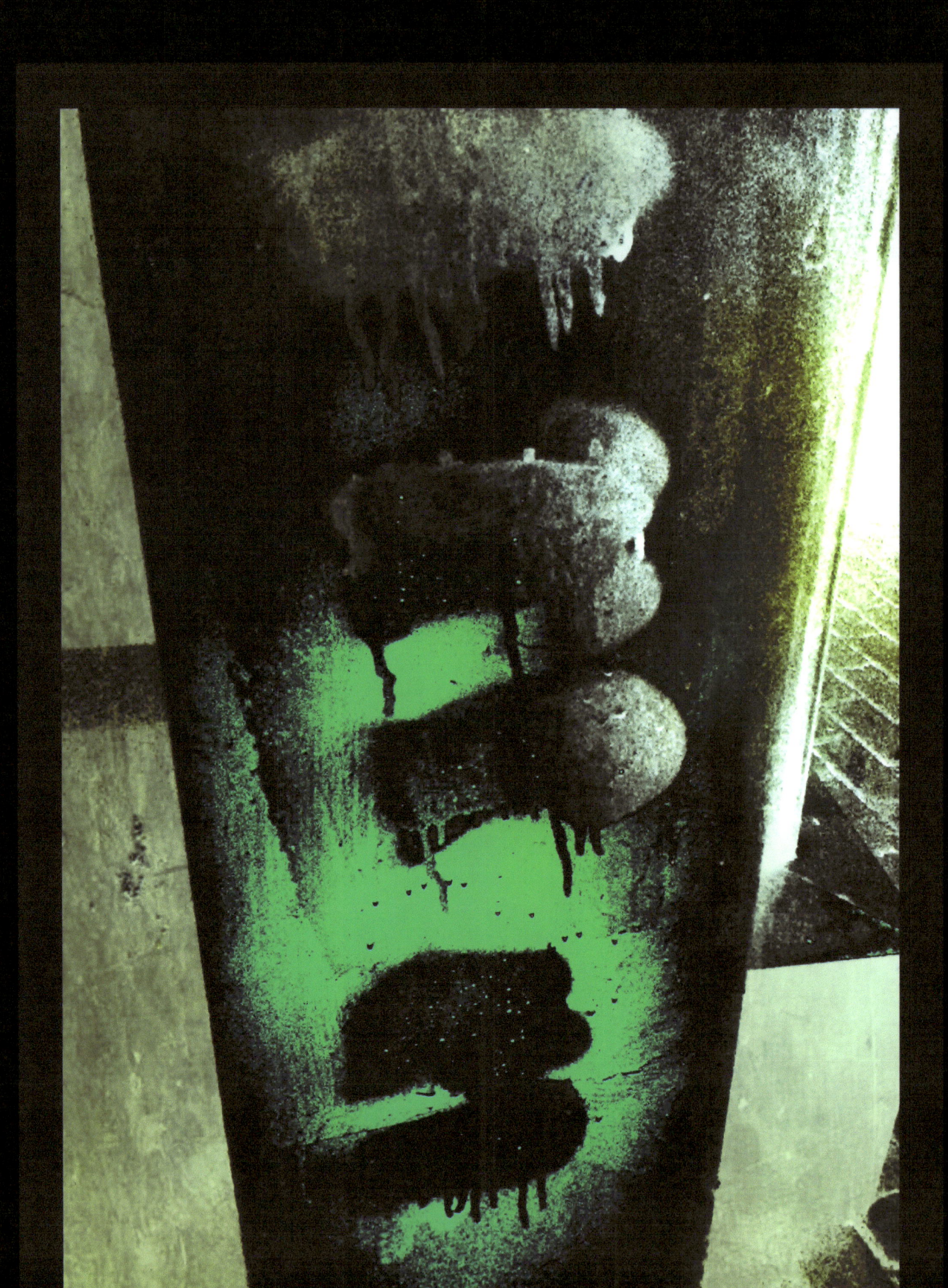

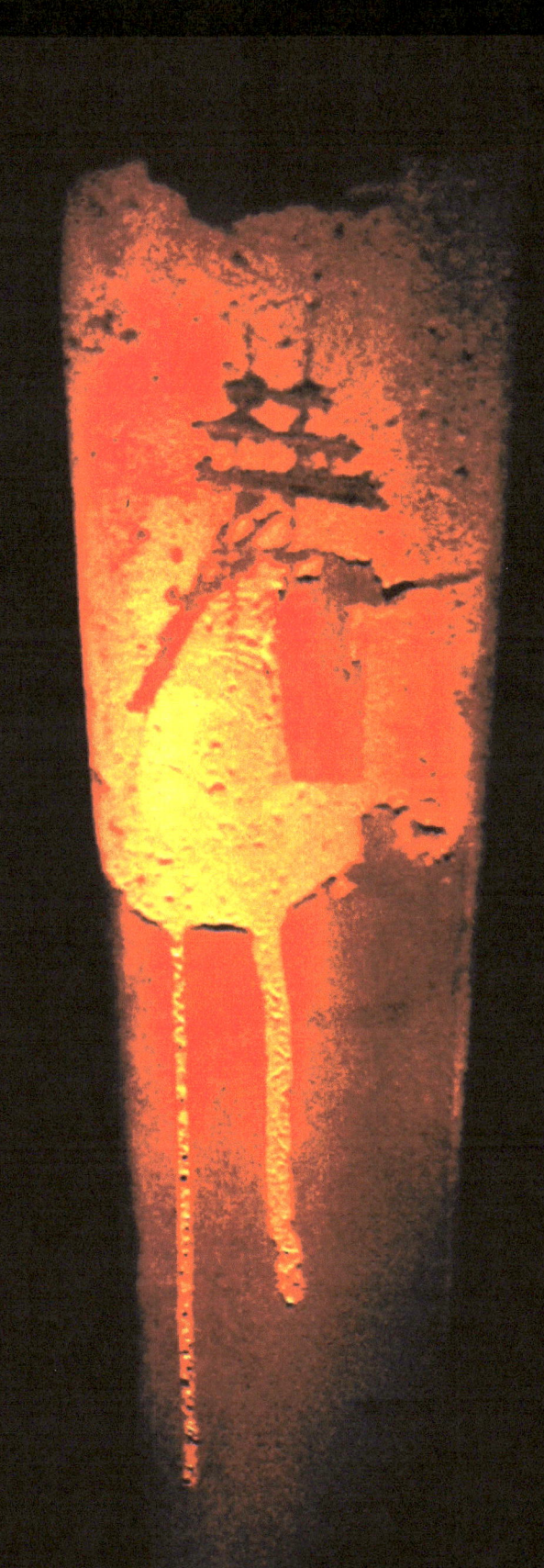

Cover me over with paint, sand and mortar. Screen away my thoughts of you through sticker ads I totter. Crimson colored etched beneath the peeling terracotta.

Engraved in stone and sand eroded, the street beneath your eyes, in day and night they forage.

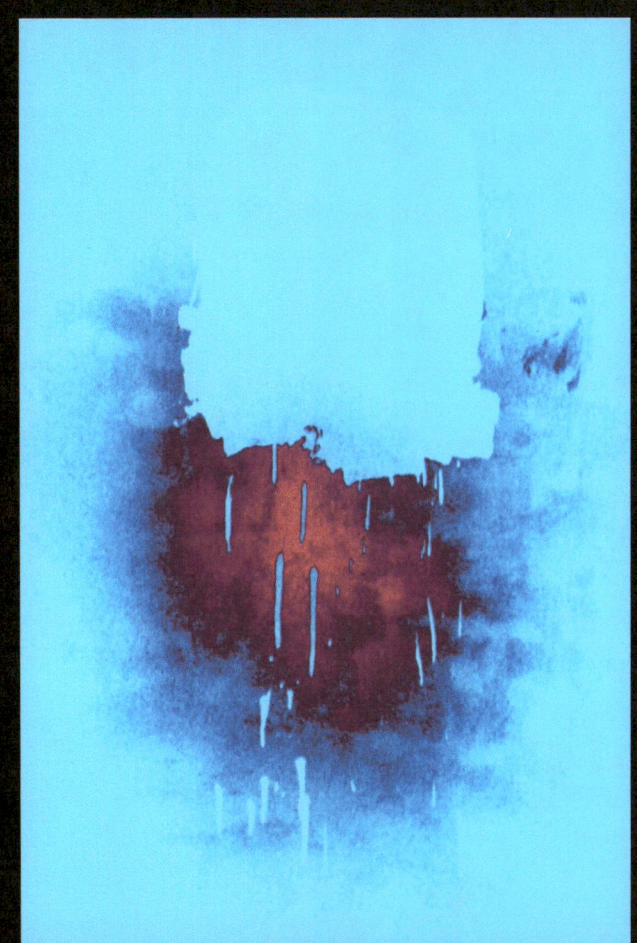

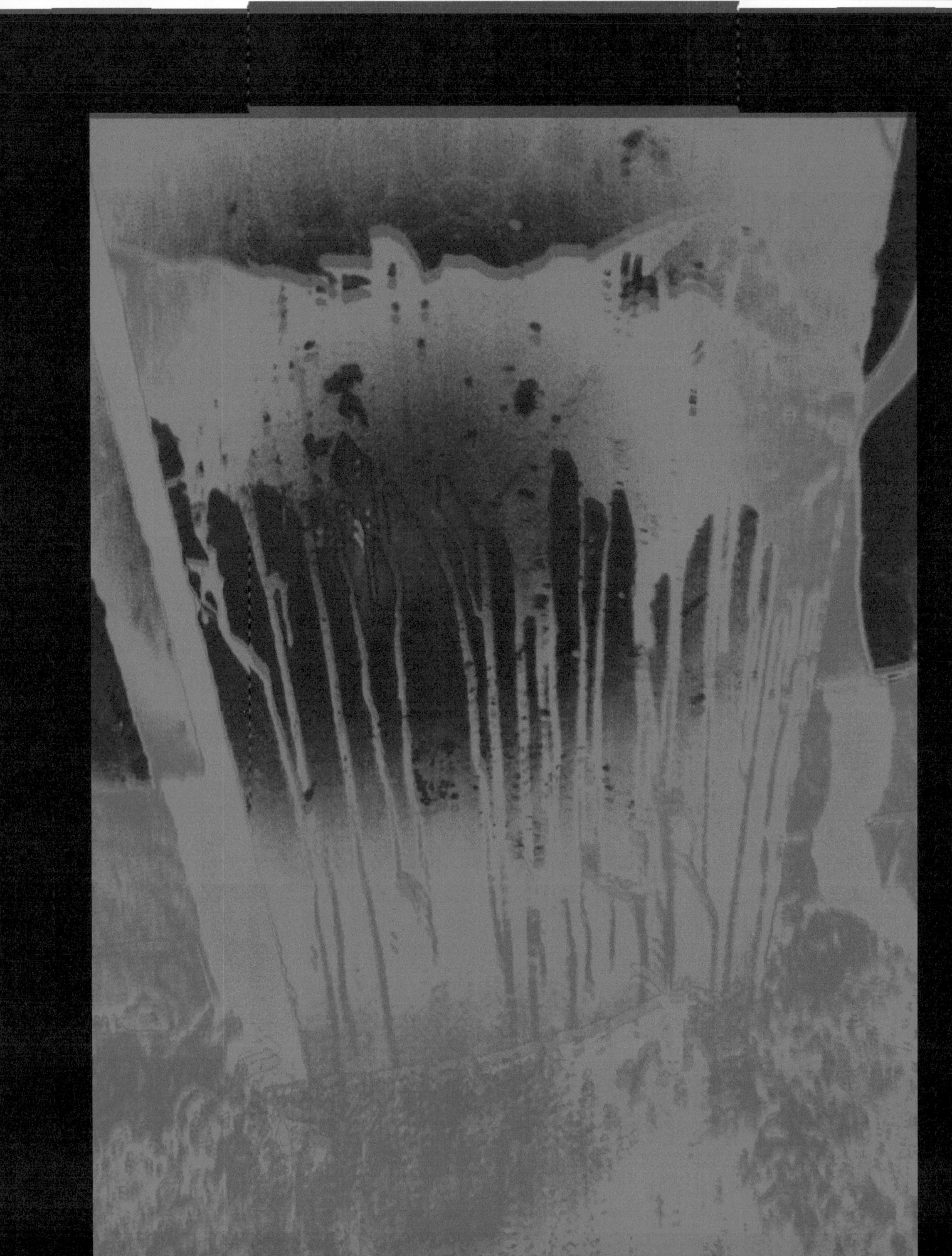

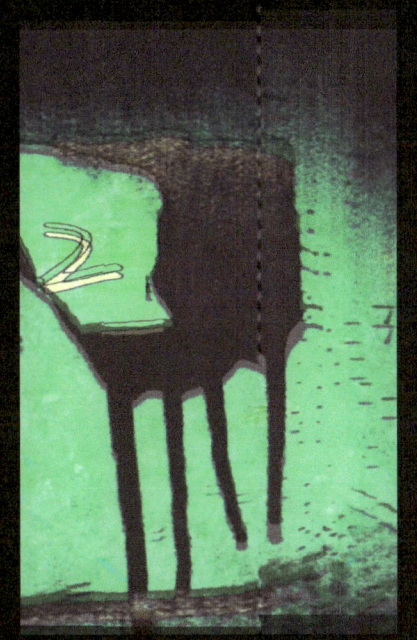

AS ONE CREATES, SO SOME SPECULATE,
IT'S NATURE THAT ONE DOES.
BUT, LIFE GENERATES AS TO ITS HABITAT
TO NURTURE, GROW AND PROSPER. EACH
TRY AT IT, IS OFTEN MET WITH GRIT, OF
SAND AND SOME OF FERVOR.
SO, DAY AND NIGHT AND NIGHT AND DAY,
THE CYCLES END IS NO MORE NEARER.

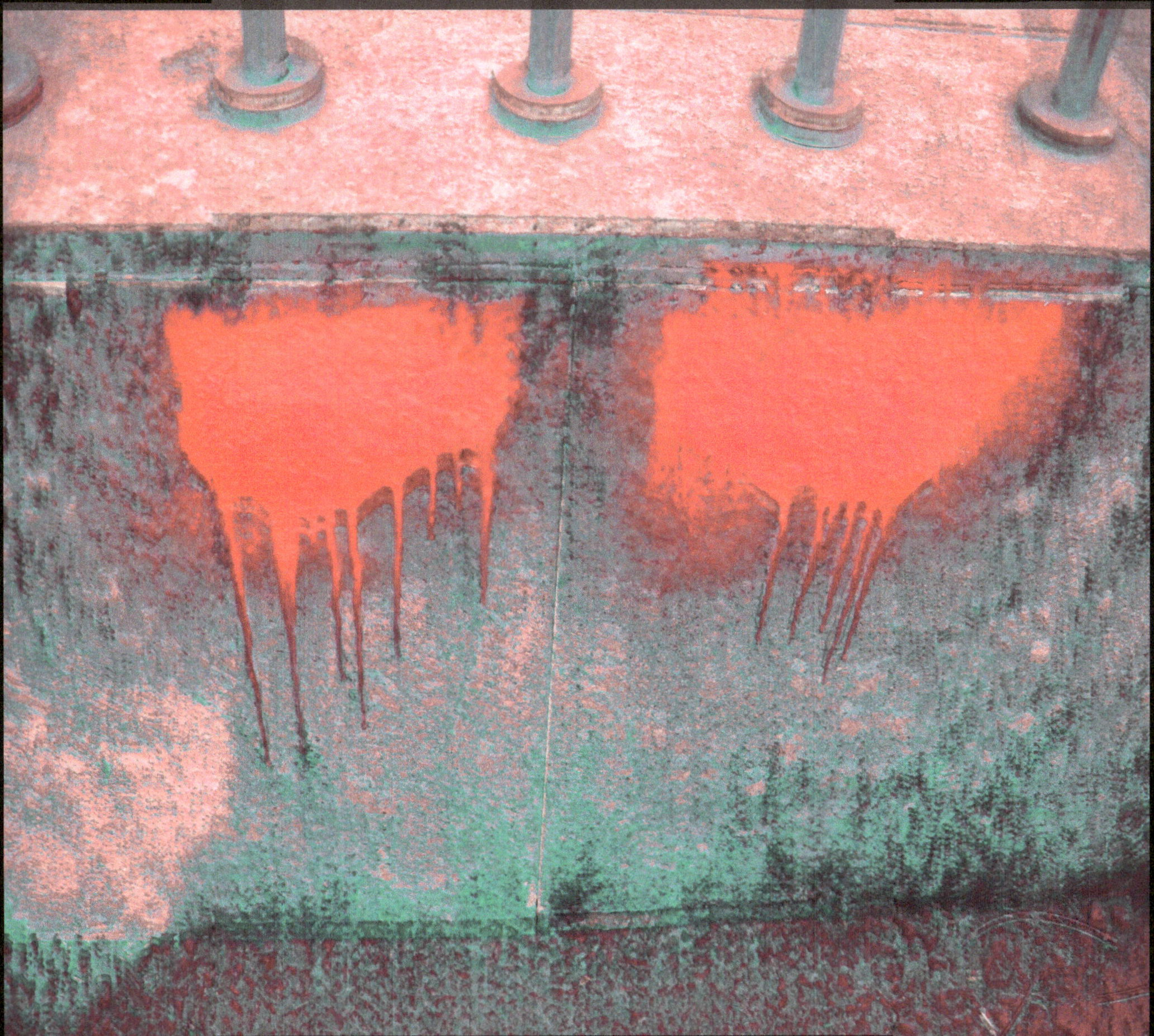

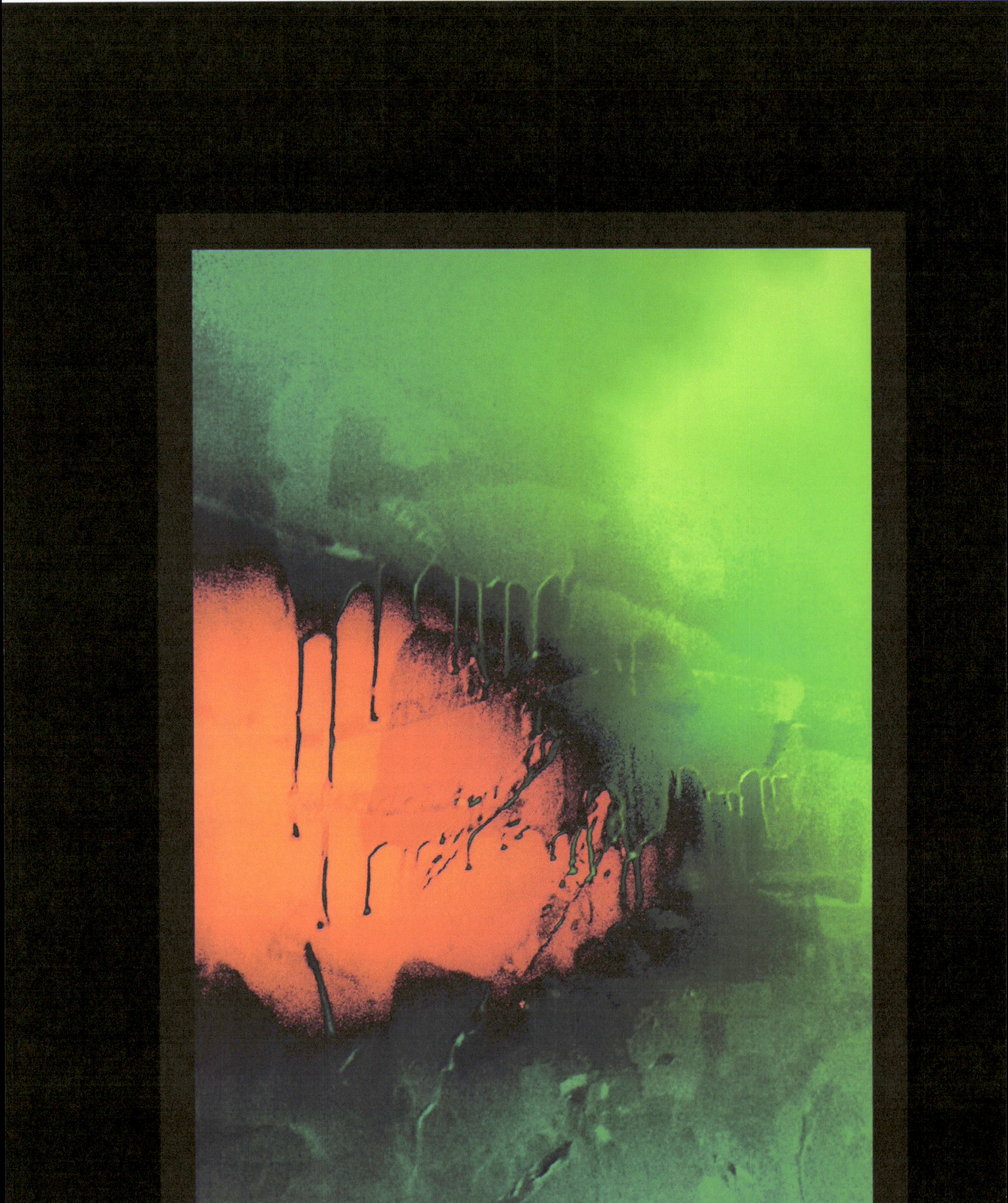

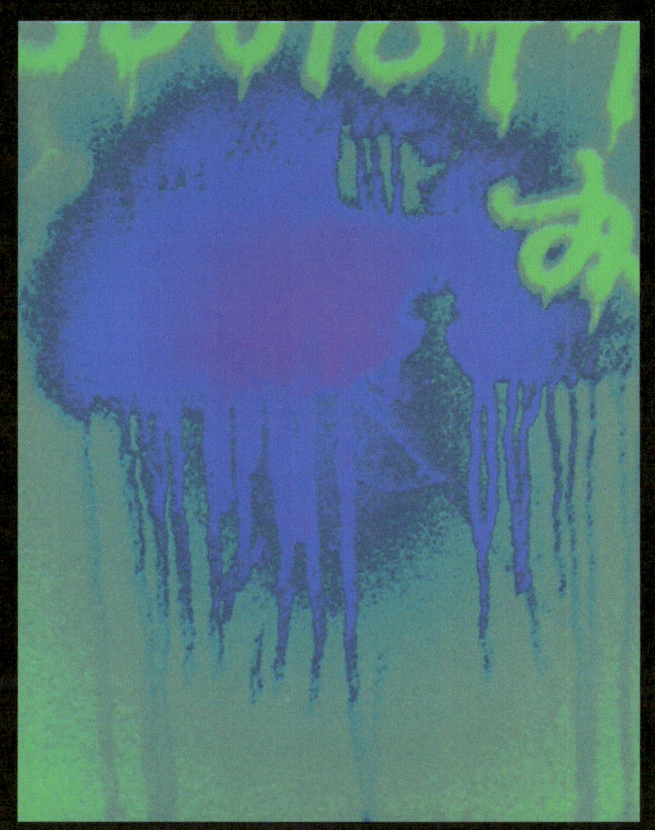
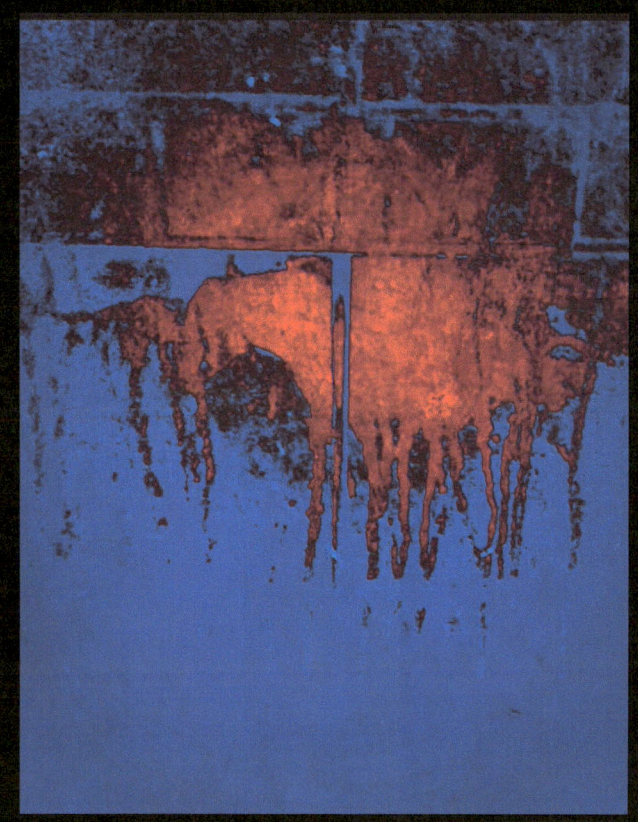
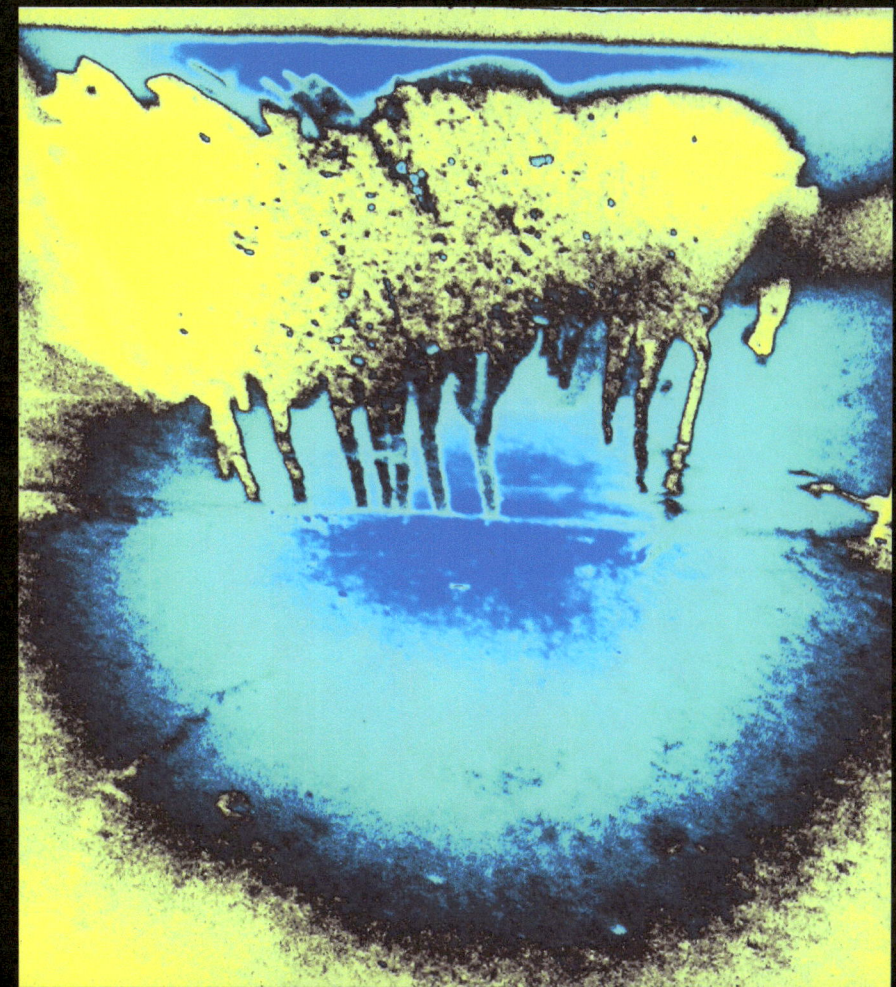

ON STEPS I SEE, ON THE TOPS AND BENEATH. AJAR I SAY. ALONG THE BACK, DOWN THE WAY. BETWEEN THE POSTS NEAR HERE. STATIONED HIGH ABOVE THERE. PARALLEL TO THE PALLETS. NEXT TO THE BIN. A MOST OVERCAST OF DAYS IT HAS BEEN.

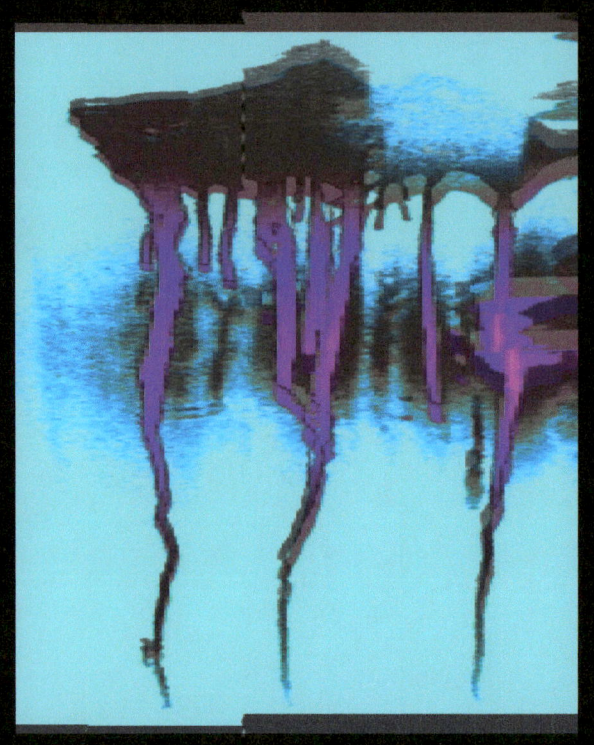
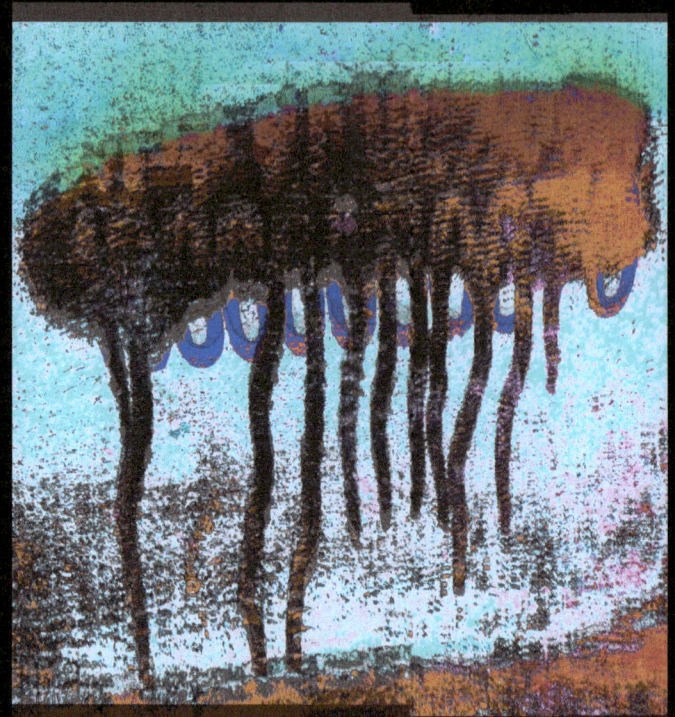

Each day anew, each day to do what one is imbued to view.

Upon brick and stone carved or herringbone one spreads its seed in hope.

Can it be? Some may intercede, that this is all a bit unruly?

But it's not of pleasure but for duty that such beauty is left to diminish.

So it's left alone to continue as such until such time as it's seen fit.

To march around with paint in hand and brush in other and go get rid of it.

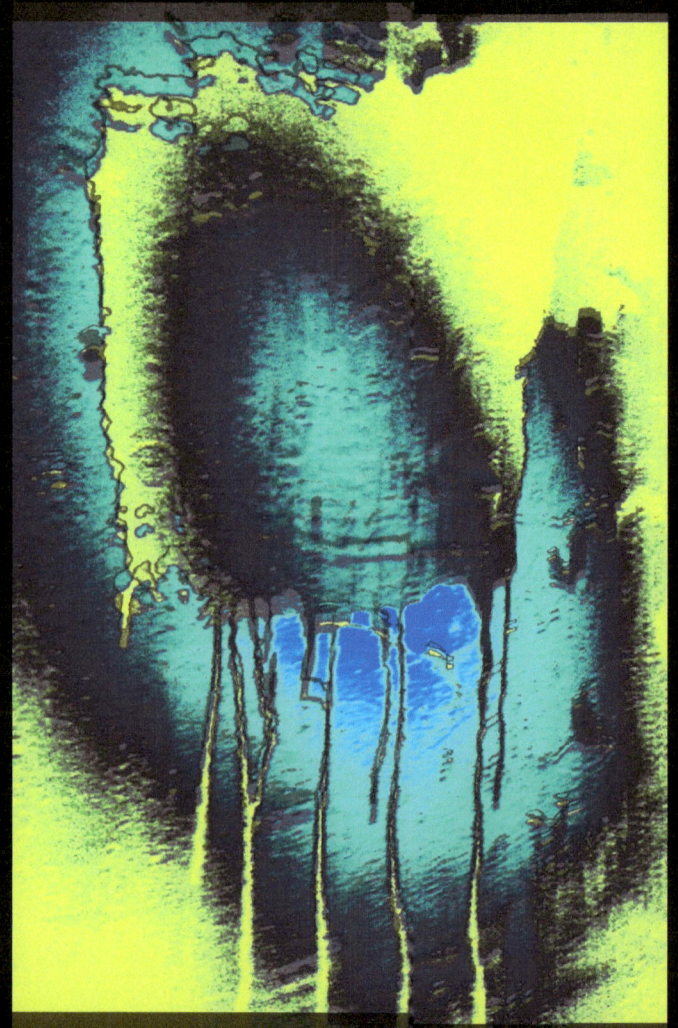

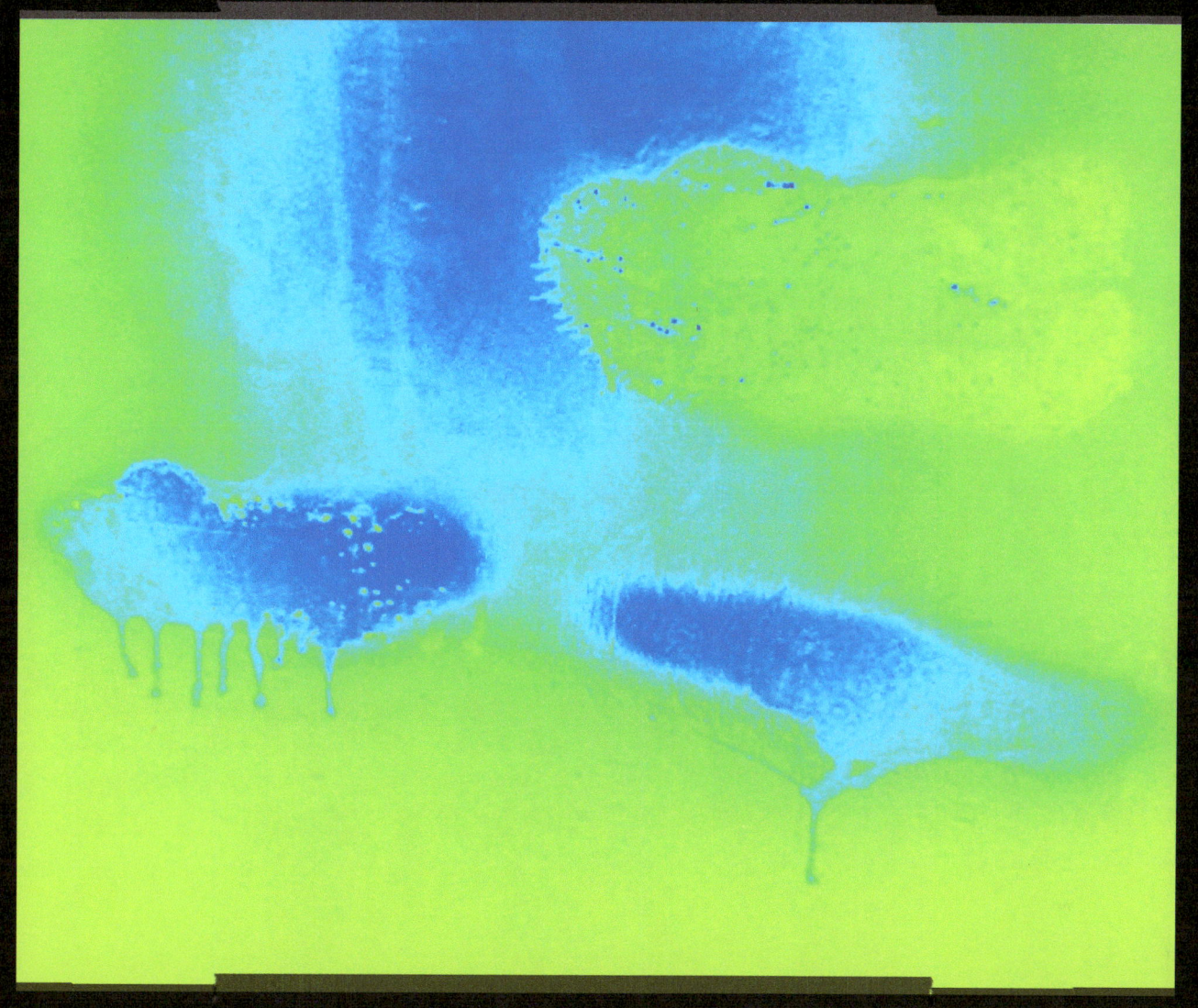

THE PAINT DRIPS DRY AS THE PAINT CHIPS FLAKE
THE PAINT CHIP CRUMBLES BENEATH THE STREET SWEEP'S WAKE
THE STREET SWEEPS HARD, THERE'S A SWEAT BEAD ON THE BROW
TO THE EARTH IT FALLS; TO THE EARTH IT HAS FALLEN
THE CLOUDS HAVE APPEARED THEN THEY WILL SOON BE GONE
TO EVERY CLOUD THAT PASSES FOR A TIME THEN RETURNS
TO EVERY HAND THAT WAS AT WORK TO GROW AND TO PLUNDER
THE URBAN CLOUDS; EYES HAVE SEEN AND CAN NEVER UNCOVER.

Conclusion

Urban Clouds was a way I processed what I was seeing around me.. It was a way I turned something that many saw as degrading and destructive into a thing of beauty.

I will always look for the good in something, the beauty under the rubble and the diamond in the rough. I found distinctions and characteristics from region to region but all shared that unmistakable cloudlike formation.

I hope this book inspires you in some shape or form to look around you and perceive meanings and create a world with color and splendor, of richness of language and song. Whatever you do, share it with the world and remember - every cloud has a silver lining.

Breeze Canyon.

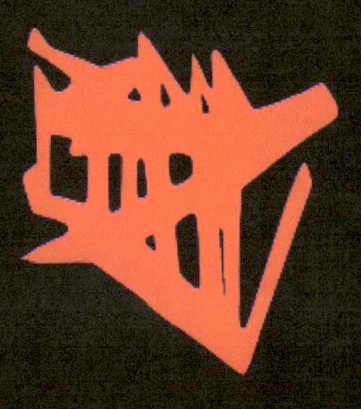

LIVE Be YOUR Original LIFE

www.ingramcontent.com/pod-product-compliance
Lightning Source LLC
Chambersburg PA
CBHW051943210526
45473CB00006B/2366